Tips to romance your Husband

Foreword by **Barbara Rainey**

FamilyLife Publishing
Little Rock, Arkansas

Simply Romantic® Tips to Romance Your Husband
 Published 2005
Printed in the United States of America

11 10 09 08 07 06 05   1 2 3 4 5 6 7

ISBN: 1-57229-720-4

Written and Edited by: Margie Clark, Amy Bradford, Fran Taylor, Gregg Stutts, and Mary Larmoyeux
Graphic Designer: Lee Smith
Illustration: Whitney Eoff
Cover Photography: Willie Allen

FamilyLife
Dennis Rainey, President
5800 Ranch Drive
Little Rock, Arkansas 72223
(501) 223-8663 • www.familylife.com

Contents

Foreword

Dry-erase markers, coupons, puzzle pieces, and chocolates … this little book is packed with innovative ideas to help you communicate love to your sweetheart.

Creatively expressing love involves forethought and planning. Let's face it, most of us could use some inspiration to spark romance—*Simply Romantic Tips to Romance Your Husband* is packed with ideas that will help you demonstrate love to your husband.

Sometimes even the smallest gesture can say, "I love you." Take the time to show him that you notice him and know what he likes. Your beloved will be encouraged … your friendship will be strengthened … and romance will be sparked.

Barbara Rainey

Barbara Rainey
Wife of Dennis Rainey, President of FamilyLife
Mother of six and grandmother of eight

Romantic Messages

Write him a check for one hundred kisses.
Be available to cash the check for him when and where he pleases.

Buy your guy a leather-bound journal and write inspirational and romantic quotes, thoughts and love notes for him. As you journey through life together, continue adding new thoughts that affirm your love and respect for him.

2

Create a special—and unusual—place in the house to make love.
Leave little Post-it® notes throughout the house leading
your husband to your special love nest.

Before your next day at the beach,
prepare a special message in a bottle for your loved one.
Hide it in a place where the two of you
will come across it as you lead him on a walk.

4

Write a message to your husband on cardstock, and cut it into five puzzle pieces. For four continuous days, mail him one of the pieces. On the fifth day reveal when and where he should meet you to get the final piece of the puzzle.

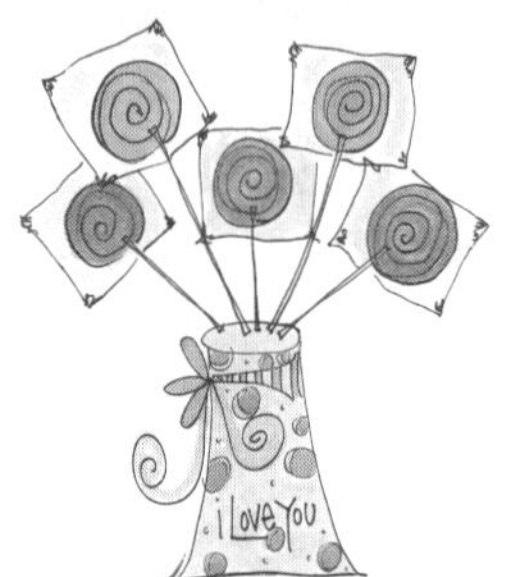

Leave a note in his car that says “I can’t wait to see you tonight” …
or maybe … ”I can’t wait for you to see me tonight?”
Then wear something to bed that catches his eye.

Send a sexy e-mail or text message to your man.

When your husband goes out of town,
give him a sealed note for each day he will be gone.
Build anticipation in each note for his return home.

8

The next time you're out to dinner, casually take out a pen and write a note to him on a paper napkin—letting him know what he can look forward to at home. Fold it and slide it across the table.

Compliment your husband in front of others.
You may be the only one in his life who's doing it!

11

Using dry-erase markers, leave a note to your sweetie on the bathroom mirror.

On a small piece of paper,
write a short note of encouragement
and slip it into his pants pocket.
He'll find it later when he's fishing for change.

12

Send a bouquet of candies or cookies to his workplace with a sweet note.

13

Compose a love poem (perhaps a haiku) for your love.
Find a special time and place to read it to him.
Consider framing it and hanging it in your bedroom.

14

Romantic Touch

Slide over and sit next to your loved one in the car.
Buckle up for safety.

Treat your hardworking honey to a backrub.

16

17

Dust off that old game of Twister® and have some fun! With each round, the loser must remove a piece of clothing. He'll be sure to see that you lose.

Join him the next time he's taking a shower. Too shy? Then greet your guy with a warm towel as he's stepping out of the shower and help him dry off.

18

As he heads out for work, give him a passionate kiss. If he wants to know what it was for—tell him it's the appetizer for tonight's menu.

Go for a walk after dinner holding hands.

Spend time kissing him—*really* kissing him.

Play footsie with him the next time you are having dinner at your in-laws.

22

When the house is quiet—light some candles—
play some soft music—and dance cheek to cheek.
Make it a dance he will never forget!

The next time your husband is at the kitchen sink, walk up behind him and give him a really big hug.

24

Pamper his tootsies with a relaxing foot massage. All you need is a warm basin of water, some soap, a towel, and some lotion.

On a chilly night, cuddle under a blanket
with your husband and watch a movie.
Surprise him with a little kiss on the lips or nip on the neck.

26

Get up a few minutes earlier than usual, brush your teeth, then get back in bed and wake him up with a kiss.

Play the "Touching Game".
Make 10 cards describing
"Ways to Touch"—and 10 cards with
"Places to Touch" (one idea per card).
Without looking, pull one card from
each pile and then take action.

Romantic Gifts

Save your spare change in a large, clear jar.
Let him know you are saving up to buy him something special.

Make him a book of coupons that are good for things he likes: his favorite dessert, a special meal, and you.

30

31

Bring him a surprise from the grocery store—
a magazine, a candy bar, or whatever else
will let him know you were thinking about him.

Buy him that CD, DVD, book,
or video game that he's had his eye on.

32

Keep a running list of his favorite things, clothes sizes and gift ideas. (See the appendix for special charts.)

33

Go with him to his favorite store—
and let him treat himself to something he'd like.

34

Secretly buy him tickets to a special event. Plan a lunch/dinner date on the day of the event. After dessert, give him the tickets.

35

Purchase a piece of clothing for yourself that you know he will especially like. Pick a special time and place to wear it!

36

If your husband is a collector of coins, baseball cards, etc., buy him something that adds to his collection.

37

Have a professional photographer take a picture of you. Frame your favorite pose and give it to your husband.

38

Refrain from saying "I told you so."
That might be the best gift of all.

39

Find a used bookstore or check online for a collectible copy of his favorite book.

40

Handwrite his favorite Bible verse on parchment. After laminating it, surprise him by tucking it into his Bible.

41

For a significant anniversary—buy him a gold watch.
Engrave it with a romantic phrase like “I’ll always have time for you.”

42

Romantic Moments

Arrange for you and your spouse to take a day off—and then do something you enjoy together.

Schedules can often get out of control. Be sure to schedule time just for yourself, so you will have some energy left for him.

44

Serve him his favorite dessert and gourmet coffee—by candlelight.

45

Take the afternoon off and catch a matinee. Sit in the back row!

46

Play a board game you both enjoy.

47

Sit down with your husband and listen to him.
Ask him how you can help fulfill the dreams he has for his life.

48

Reminisce about your favorite dating memories. Plan together to reproduce his favorite one.

Pick up the book *Rekindling the Romance* and tell him you'd like to read it together.

50

Go to a local park.
Spend some time reconnecting as a couple.
Pack snacks and stay awhile.

Have your guy write down on slips of paper his five favorite things to do. Fold them and place them in a bowl. Let him draw one out and read it—then do it together.

Circle and star a location on a map,
then tape the map to the fridge. When he asks,
just smile and wink—but don't tell.
On the appointed day, drive him to the location
and either have a picnic or just make out.

Play a spicy rendition of the old classic childhood game of "Mother May I?". Change the name to "Darling May I?" and have lots of grown up fun.

54

Blindfold your husband and "kidnap" him. Take him to a hotel room where you have prepared a romantic tryst.

Take a class together. Find a topic, hobby, or sport you both want to learn more about—and sign up!

56

Spend time together in the kitchen making his favorite dinner, cookies, or dessert.

57

Prepare a special snack at bedtime—and serve it to him in bed. Chocolate covered anything is sure to please!

58

Romantic Moves

Wash and vacuum his car.
For the final touch—top off his gas tank, too.

Make an effort to keep yourself healthy and physically fit.

Pick up his favorite dish from his favorite restaurant and serve it to him on your best china.

61

Host a party for him and his friends
to watch their favorite sporting event on TV.

62

Give him a break from his weekend chores by either mowing the lawn or arranging for it to be done.

63

Drop by your husband's workplace unexpectedly and whisk him away for lunch.

64

Initiate something special in the bedroom.

You are never too old to flirt. Flirt with the man you married.

66

Surprise your husband with a special "spa treatment" after he's had a long, hard day at work. Draw him a bath and create a soothing environment—scented candles, bubbles, music, refreshing beverage, etc.

Think of a couple of things that your honey does for you and the family (he is a good provider, he can fix things, etc.) and let him know how much you appreciate him.

68

On Friday night—tell him he gets to sleep in late the next morning.
Serve him breakfast in bed.

Offer to shave him. (If you think there is any chance you might accidentally cut him, then skip this one.)

70

Plan a weekend away for the two of you.
Cater to his desires and his needs.

The next time he's watching a game on television,
ask him if he has any plans for halftime.
If not, tell him you've made plans for him to score.

72

Prepare for special events:
Maintain current e-mail addresses and cell phone numbers of your husband's friends. You may want to throw him a surprise birthday party or plan a celebration when he accomplishes something significant.

Hire a handy man to fix things around the house. Use the time you saved your hubby to do something fun together.

74

Romantic Advice

If your lives are crazy busy—
schedule some special time for romance on your calendars.
Use little red heart stickers to mark the days.

Men are stimulated by sight—
take a personal interest in your appearance.

76

Seek to resolve misunderstandings and conflict before you go to sleep each night.

Admit when you're wrong and be willing to say, "I'm sorry, will you forgive me?"

78

Consider attending a Weekend to Remember® marriage conference. Visit www.familylife.com.

Remember:
"The older the violin, the sweeter the music."
(author unknown)

81

Ladies—shave your legs before you go to bed.

Instead of feeling frustrated when he forgets to put the toilet seat down—thank him when he remembers.

82

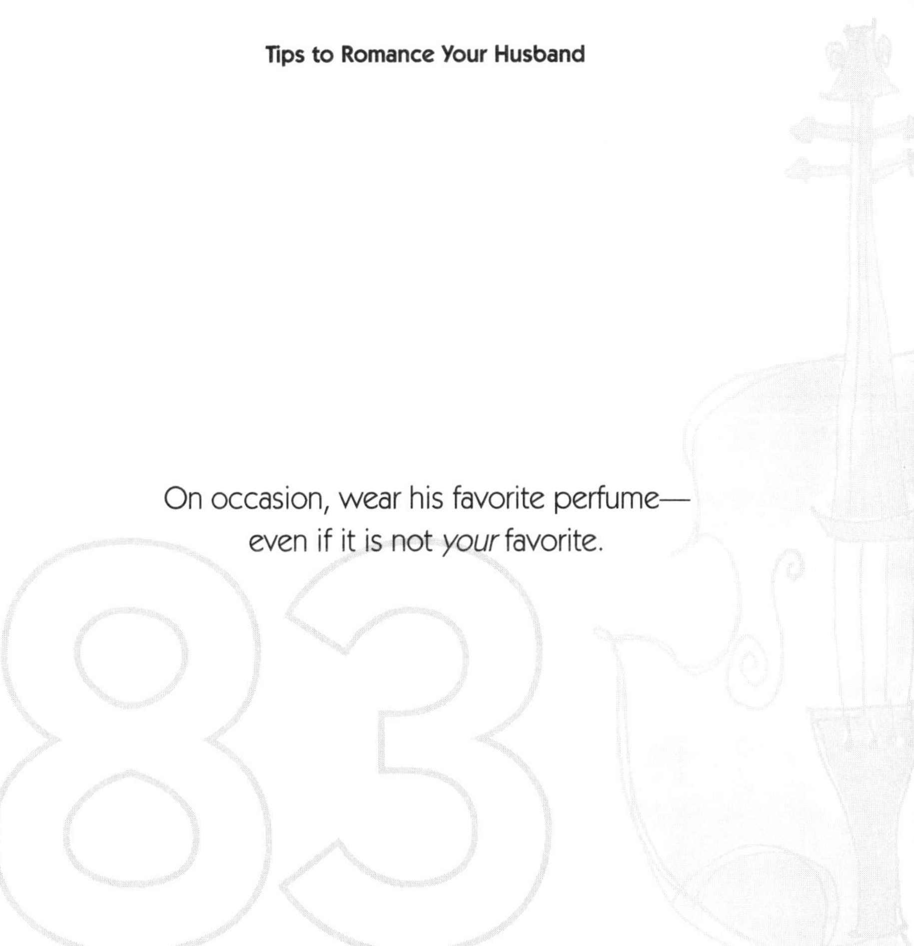

On occasion, wear his favorite perfume—
even if it is not *your* favorite.

Be a student of your spouse. Know his likes and dislikes, his strengths and weaknesses, and his fears.

84

Keep your romance closet well stocked with candles, greeting cards, massage oil, bubble bath, chocolate, etc.

85

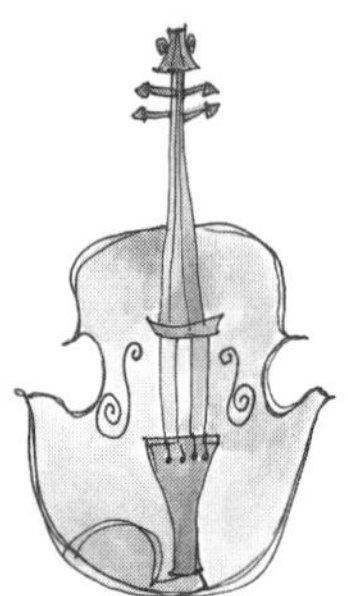

Men view romance differently from women.
Ask your husband to describe what's romantic to him.
Don't be surprised when his ideas sound very different from yours.

86

Pray for your husband every day.

Romantic Holidays and Special Days

88

In this New Year, whisper in his ear that you are determined to find some new places to kiss him. When you're alone with him, start to make good on your promise.

Fill several Easter eggs with notes telling your husband why you love him. Nestle the eggs in a decorated basket.

89

The next time you and your spouse attend a wedding—tell him "If I had it to do all over, I'd marry you again." Enjoy a second honeymoon after the reception.

90

Have fun foolin' around on April Fool's Day. Share an umbrella, roll up your jeans, and splash in the puddles *sans galoshes.*

91

Tell your husband that you will be treating him to an off-season baseball game for Valentine's Day. Then, in your bedroom or some other private location, lead him through first base, second base, third base, and then bring him in for a home run.

92

Celebrate his birthday at the office
with cake and ice cream for everyone.

93

Sleep in, have breakfast in bed, and watch the Groundhog Day prediction together. If the groundhog sees his shadow, unveil your six-week plan for staying warm.

94

The 19th of October is Sweetest Day.
Ask his mother to list his favorite candies from childhood.
Purchase these nostalgic goodies as a special gift for your sweetie.

95

On Thanksgiving Day, give him a handwritten letter with the reasons you are thankful that he is in your life.

96

Send your mate on a treasure hunt this Columbus Day. Slip him a map that will lead him through a series of clues to his ultimate treasure - you.

97

98

Spice-up the "Twelve Days of Christmas." Each day from December 25 through January 5 create small, personal gifts (notes, snacks, yourself!) for him only.
January 6 buy a King's Cake, or make your own, to close out the Christmas season.

Father's Day is a great day to celebrate with your husband. Rent a convertible for the day and drive around with the top down.

99

100

Plan a romantic birthday surprise.
Book the honeymoon suite at your favorite hotel,
and buy him a special gift—
something that reveals your birthday suit.

Make your own holiday! Take this opportunity to create a holiday that is special and unique to the two of you.

101

Acknowledgments

We want to thank the following people for their contributions to *Simply Romantic Tips to Romance Your Husband:*

FamilyLife staff and visitors to www.familylife.com, Sabrina Beasley, Amy Bradford, Margie Clark, Eric Dahinden, Hugh Duncan, Dan Gaffney, Marcie Hefner, Kathy Harrill, Sharon Hill, Nicole Kinzler, Phil Krause, Cindy Landes, Mary Larmoyeux, Marla Livers, Julie Majors, Todd Nagel, Jenni Smith, John Stokes, Gregg Stutts, Suzanne Thomas, and Denise Truelove.

Appendix

Jeans: ____________________

Slacks: ____________________

Shirt: ____________________

Shoes: ____________________

Ring: ____________________

Other: ____________________

____

Gift list: